T0148610

A Breath Of Rhyme

Barbara DiLorenzo-McCormick

Order this book online at www.trafford.com
or email orders@trafford.com

Most Trafford titles are also available at major online book retailers.

Printed in the United States of America.

ISBN: 978-1-4669-5665-0 (sc)
ISBN: 978-1-4669-5666-7 (e)

Trafford rev. 09/04/2012

   www.trafford.com

North America & international
toll-free: 1 888 232 4444 (USA & Canada)
phone: 250 383 6864 ♦ fax: 812 355 4082

Deception

Beware, the snake that never sleeps,
Lurking, cautiously, he is waiting,
Within the grass temptation creeps,
Beware, creatures that prowl the night,
Marking time to absorb fresh blood,
Unbroken his sinful appetite,
Picking the flowers not yet in bud,
Wandering unaware of life and the cruelness,
Resting unsure, the still of darkness,
Beware the fruit, said to be forbidden
Sweet to the lips, but bitter the taste,
Behind a smile danger is hidden,
Gentle eyes, with contempt his thoughts are laced
And his twisted tongue, will only seem to make sense,
Beware wounds, that tend to deepen,
Baited by the devil in disguise,
Virtue the prey prone to weaken,
In this garden of truth and lies,
The serpent lies scheming, with his hand held out,
Confusing all who have suspicion or doubt

Angel

I wish to be an angel,
But I do not wish to die,
I would like a pair of wings,
Even if I can't fly,
I want to do what is good,
And believe in what is right,
I I want to see everything,
Through the shine of heavens light,
I want to rise above,
Maybe sit on a cloud,
I hope to see all who passed,
Standing out in a crowd,
I want to be an angel,
With eyes that glow,
Questions without asking,
Answers among wisdom to know,

I want to have a sense,
Beyond all being,
To come into endless view,
Blessed with the ability of a foreseeing.

Quiet

When it is quiet,
There is only thought,
When there is nothing left,
To be sold or bought,
A shaking calm,
Haas overcome,
Leaving behind everything,
What is done is done,
A love that could,
Or could never be,
Why did you,
Do this to me,
Now it is quiet,
Before the storm,
Holding the rose,
Punctured by its thorn,
Everything familiar,
Everything I know,
I open my hand,
And let it go.

Sis

When no one is there,
You always come through,
Don't know how I didn't see it,
But now . . . , now I do,
You always make me laugh,
Even when I want to cry,
We share something in the heart,
Beyond sisters tie,
When I think of you,
And what you've done for me,
If I had to give it back,
It would take an eternity,

How thankful I am to you,
I could never explain,
Because I have the best big sister,
I LOVE you Loraine.

Purpose

Desires for pleasure,
Constantly fighting within,
Called out of the darkness,
To play with sin,
Angel of death,
Demon of agony,
Have some mercy,
Show a little sympathy,
Silence the ignorant,
By doing what is good,
Remembering the words spoken,
Are like fire to wood,
Through the whole being,
The course of existence,
Fighting the tears,
The tears of resistance,
How much more,
In that which last forever,
Its faith, hope, and patience,
Never failing, failing never,
To this very moment,
Expose the hidden,
The purpose of the mind,
What is allowed and what is forbidden.

I Can Feel

I can feel your breath,
On my ear,
Your body is pressed against mine,
Right here,
Slightly touching,
Finger tips,
Softly sucking on both,
Your lips,

I can feel the strength,
Of your embrace,
As you slide your hand,
Across my face,
I can feel your breath,
On me everywhere,
I can feel . . . , I can feel,
But there is no one there.

Spiral

The screaming has ceased,
A lingering fear,
A betrayal of calm,
Wondering why I am here,
To sleep without slumber,
The eyes afraid to close,
Wisdom comes to sparkle,
Punctured releasing the rose,
Obscurity blinking, falling,
Descending within a black and white spiral,
People say the passion I put into what I do,
Is far above normal,
The screams have ceased,
As doubt is at surrender,
God is LOVE,
Within what is tender.

Daddy

His picture hangs,
Over his bed,
The body beneath,
Lies lifeless and dead,
Daddy don't go,
Take a breath,
Don't leave me here to deal with death,
Daddy . . . , don't go,
The end is near,
What happened to the man,
In that picture there,

Once so strong,
Now so weak,
Disease has made,
The future bleak,
Daddy . . . . , don't go,
It's the knowing I can't take,
To see you this way,
Has caused me also to ache,
Daddy . . . . , Daddy,
Tears are making hard to see,
I know you feel it too,
Daddy, please don't leave me.

The Wind

The wind it whispers,
As it goes by,
The rain it pours,
As tears to cry,
Looking around emptiness,
The ground is calling,
Beneath the dirt,
Life is falling,
Feeling more alone,
With every day that passes,
From dust to dust,
Dreams are only ashes,
Like the sky without a cloud,
Not shaded emotions burn,
Surrounded by elements,'
Showing little or no concern,
Aware the road isn't,
The only thing being crossed,
Its true you need not travel,
To be in the middle of nowhere lost,
Finding no comfort in time,
Youth is consumed by age,
While disease is unpredictable,
As a storm in rage,
Withering away as any building or tree,
The wind it whispers . . . . whispers to me.

Embellish

Like sheep to a shepherd,
Impelling each word,
Pertaining to sacred,
Undermine until dead,
A servant on a journey,
In fact perplexity,
To embellish the tragic,
Superficial, caustic,
Casting gloom upon,
To accept then abandon.

Adorn

Within the edges,
Exists a center,
Doors meant,
To exit and enter,
The distant hum of music,
Simple, free unbroken,
A beggar with purpose to bleed,
Passing overcast adorn awaken,
To reach deep within beauty,
A spirit to infringe upon,
Into the burden of concept,
While love, love beckons,
Dark good fortune,
By design,
The atmosphere sings,
Modest passion of mine,
In mid-air groundless,
Sabatage brutal palliate,
Dwelling heavily the critical,
While the superficial visions illuminate.
Mist
My eyes fill with tears,
But I won't cry,
I hold back my breath,
Until the feeling goes by,

I wait for an answer,
Each time I pray,
I'll have the strength and faith,
To get through another day,
My eyes glare with tears,
But I will be alright,
I'll swallow the hurt,
With each and every bite,
I'll wait for an angel,
Some sign from heaven,
Realizing I'm alone,
No . . . , not again,
My eyes fill with tears,
But I refuse to let them fall,
I will hold them back,
Rather than risk it all,
I will wait because I know,
My God is near,
I'll wait . . . , I'll wait . . . ,
In the mist of a tear.

Brass Rail

Inside this brass rail lonely faces can be found,
With each sip, deeper sorrow is drowned,
Watch the action hear no sound,
Surrounded in a friendless surrender of the night.
Cold is the soul drifting without a destiny,
Feel the hurt of another forsaken heart left empty,
As lips mumble words unconsciously,
Visions become unaware of deceiving sight,
As I observe people who step through these doors of corruption,
At the next table they slowly lose control of reflection,
While others wash down love mistaken for desperation,
Here is to the smile acquired to delude,
Leaving behind a doubtful stain,
Spending a moment in time to elude,
As a hidden haze of tears lingers in the atmosphere,
Through these eyes I see the darkness of despair,
Pulling up another chair . . . .

Shhh

Shhh . . . . , don't wake,
Those memories,
The ones refused,
Refused to see,
The picture hidden,
Somewhere inside,
Thoughts blocked out,
Finding a place to hide,
What could disturb,
All that is normal or known,
Waking what is dead,
Not wanting to be alone,
Something off balance,
And lingers within,
Not even thought,
Is safe from its sin,
Shhh . . . . , its asleep,
And that's where it will stay,
Until it is awakened,
To take you away.

It Calls

It calls to me from,
The depth of my heart,
It leaves me broken,
Even torn apart,
Like an unanswered prayer,
Echoing in the night,
Leaving an indent of my hands,
From holding them so tight,
It calls to me,
So just I can hear,
Like a knock on the door,
And when you answer no ones there,
It keeps me sheltered,
But never warm,
It will throw me out,
In the worst storm,
It keeps me where,

It wants me to be,
And I'm unable,
To break free.

Come

Come steal a moment.
Within me,
Rub against my flesh,
Passionately,
Fathom beyond,
The darkened sky,
While I cause your lips,
Desired reply,
Emerging into one anothers,
Heart-beat,
Entwined in passions music,
Conforming complete,
Come . . . . , come . . . ,
But only in vision,
Confined not further than,
The moments prison.

Crash

It's my fault,
I lost control,
I drove my car,
Right into that pole,
I tried to break,
I tried to swerve,
But I could not see,
Around the curve,
I remember how,
It was hard to stop,
I wanted to . . . ,
But defenses drop,
It's my fault,
I said go slow,
Yet pressed the gas,
When better I know,
I'm not hurt,

Just a little shaken,
Thought it was more,
But must have been mistaken.

Live

It's just a metaphor,
Of the mind,
Desolate areas,
Resting confined,
Whispers of faith,
Sorrow weeping at the door,
As an addiction wanting more,
Copiuos with exactness,
An untamed force,
Passion perceptive,
The cavity in which,
The heart beats to live.

Kevin

His name is Kevin,
He is seven,
He gives me joy,
This baby boy,
How he loves . . . , loves to talk,
One day he climbed Jacks bean stalk,
Up and up to the top,
And off a branch he did drop,
He went to find a golden egg,
But instead bumped into a giants leg,
He turned and ran back to fast,
In a sigh of relief said, "Ahh home at last".

Need

Praying is not only for,
When you are in need,
And love has nothing,
To do with greed,

While for our sins,
Jesus continues to bleed,
With the promise of doing,
What is right to succeed,
As on the innocent,
Violence will feed,
In search of those,
Easiest to mislead,
The payment is pain,
Unaware of the deed,
Though light moves,
Twice this speed,
Through good and bad,
Life will proceed,
It is lessons in life,
Meant to heed,
Still weeping,
Within an empty need,
Kills and devours,
For mercy the plead.

Waits

A tear waits at the,
Edge of an eye,
Searching for reasons,
Not to cry,
Swallowing breath,
That air won't let by,
Life wants to live,
Death is to die,
Who am I,
To question why,
Falling again and again,
Dust it off try and try,
Like talking to God,
Waiting for a reply,
Only angels . . . . ,
Angels can fly,
With a desire to know,
What wisdom can supply,
Somewhere in a dream,
Sings the music of a lullaby,

Reaching the heavens,
Up so high,
As a tear waits at the edge,
Of an eye,
Searching for reasons,
Not to cry.

Perfect

I want to be an angel,
But I am feeling so weak,
I have no rights,
No reason to speak,
I am what I am,
And do what I do,
In my defense,
How perfect are you?

Delirium

I'm not a loser,
Not a winner,
I try to be good,
Because it's easier to be a sinner,
Don't flatter me,
Don't put me down,
In your words,
I won't drown,
Don't always pay attention,
Don't always neglect,
Though at times carried away,
By the effect,
I'm not totally lost,
But not easily found,
Close to the earth,
Have my feet on the ground,
Don't tell me I'm wrong,
When no one is truly right,
You can't convince me of colors,
When there is only black and white,
Don't tell me I'm late,

I can see the time,
We all have faults,
Don't consider it a crime,
Not saying I'm smart,
Not saying I'm dumb,
Somewhere in the middle of,
Sanity and delirium.

Wind

Once I drifted upon a cloud,
Gliding across this colored bow,
To find forever further to know,
Peacefully moving to where the sky is blue,
My faith and love shines clearly true,
Rising above gray pillows of storm,
I reach for the sun hoping to stay warm,
Falling from the atmosphere as a drop of rain,
Unaware of when the wind will take me back again.

R.I.P. Love

May love rest in peace,
Right here where it lies,
May love rest in peace,
Without reason to apologize,
Place the flowers,
Where once stood,
The bride and groom,
Dig a hole,
Deep and wide,
For the one who,
Wasn't satisfied,
May love rest in peace,
And never be again,
How could something so good,
Cause such pain,
Push the dirt,
Onto the coffin,
Where love lies,
Here within,

Place the stone,
Onto its grave,
With all the years,
And memories to save,
Let's mourn love,
And all its sorrow,
For you and I,
Hands were only to borrow.

Connect

In the beginning Love was an unexpected mystery,
Overwhelmed by the way two hearts connect,
They remember their loss of gravity,
Now time has rendered the equal amount of respect,
As the years have forsaken its discovery,
Asking one another where is the fairness and intellect,
Or were we just to blind to see,
Watching love fade in the air from neglect,
Looking for reasons to question each others personality,
No longer saving articles to recollect,
As our touch looses it's sensitivity
The enigma of emotions disconnect.

Bible

I carry this book,
Where ever I go,
It is all I need,
It is all I know,
This book I hold tight,
When I am happy, when I weep,
Since I received this book at confirmation,
It has been by my side even when I sleep,
The only book over and over,
I have ever read,
Within my heart,
These words written forever Imbed.

Hear

Oh my God,
I'm drowning in despair,
Sweet Jesus,
Please answer my prayer,
When I look around,
There is no one there,
Who will listen,
Who will care,
I have nothing,
But words of sorrow to share,
How compline for love,
To be there,
Consumed by each,
Relentless tear,
Though there is,
Worse to compare,
From every sadness,
Beseeching in the air,
For every whisper,
Meant for You to hear,
The broken hearts,
Torn in fear,
Have mercy on all,
To whom You hold dear,
Solely in Your name to me,
Oh Lord please stay near.

Laughter

Disturbing darkness,
Covering the light,
Wrapped up in wrong,
Uncovering the right,
It's all a dream,
Some kind of mistake,
This hurts so much,
Every emotion aches,
Darkness devours,
Filling reality,
Unhappiness calls,

Without sympathy,
Hold that breath,
Close those eyes,
A place where,
No one hears the cries,
Disturbing darkness,
Stays so close,
Keep it hidden,
So nobody knows,
Darkness devours,
Happily ever after,
While sadness lives,
Where there was once laughter.

Undermine

I can't eat, I can't sleep,
Obscurity runs much too deep,
Similar to a chance, taking a leap,
To fade-out not to perish,
Without error to finish,
Living in the accuracy of lavish,
As the heart and soul combine,
Words leading within compline,
Cautious of those who undermine.

Rumble

Beneath the rumble,
In the sky,
Hidden within,
The human eye,
A kiss holds,
What exists within,
The soul passes like a shadow,
Between each layer of skin,
Born helpless and weak,
Dark places without breath,
Nowhere to run,
But towards death,
Knowledge too deep,
Among forsaking the pain,

Haunting like the wind,
From insanity to sane,
A stranger once known,
Vanish as a dream,
Understand you must,
Driven to the extreme,
Beneath the flash,
Of its lights,
That bounces from the clouds,
Following the stars into this night.

Tossed

Desolate in a room,
Bounded by dreams,
Loneliness lingers
Exposed to awakened screams,
Held in the hand,
Life has dealt,
So much for words,
And passion felt,
Crying out against,
Pushed forward to be denied,
When all that has worth,
Has been cast to subside,
Traverse through darkness and away.

A Force

I am a thunder bolt,
From the sky,
A strength, a force,
That doesn't die,
I am me,
Like no other,
I can sex you up love you down,
And to three children still be a mother,
I am dynamite,
When it blows,
What I accomplish next,
Nobody really knows,
At times I can be a mess,

From lifting weights to digging in the dirt,
Or I can clean it up,
Wearing heels and a skirt,
I am the rumble,
Before the light,
I'm not perfect,
But in the end do what is right,
I do my own hair,
Everything including my nails are real,
I believe in God with a deep devotion,
Helping me to write into words what I feel,
I am a thunder bolt,
From the sky,
A strength, a force,
That never dies.

Crest Fallen

The echo of evening song,
Crest fallen restrain,
From beginning to end,
Impelling to pertain,
Beyond doubt,
An unbending quest,
A tigress,
Untamed at best.

Pages

As pages in the wind,
Life passes by,
Everyone has a story to tell,
A reason to laugh and or cry,
Expecting interuption,
In everything that aspires to get done,
Close to a vesper said from ambiance,
To the ascent of the sun,
As pages in the wind,
The terrestrial sphere it turns,
Nothing is protected from sin,
And fashion in which it burns,
Expecting emotion,

Lost in loves relentless promise,
Like the passion connected,
Within the first weakened kiss,
As pages in the wind,
They are elevated to cease,
Then up thrown again and again,
Until the flutters next release.

Teen Pregnancy

She is never home,
Always out,
So much to overcome,
So much to doubt,
Always feeling short,
There's not enough,
Holding onto whatever,
Comes along,
Afraid to be alone,
How is that strong,
She is never home,
Always out,
Screaming when,
There is no reason to shout,
It's all an act,
Words are fake,
Blaming everyone,
For what she calls a mistake,
She is always out,
Never home,
A heart unsettled,
Can only roam.

Roads

Roads once familiar,
Become strange,
To progress in life,
There must be change,
Living in a world,
That forever turns,
Depending upon,

What one learns,
Greeting what is new,
Has left the word good bye,
Was it not worth,
The time and effort used to try,
While not having,
Drives every desire,
Unable to have what,
Thought can only admire.

Aloof

Pushing the pain aloof,
Pulling in the tears I would've cried,
Overwhelmed, unsure,
Nowhere to hide,
Left in a mess of emotion,
Falling, falling,
Right and wrong,
Conflict constantly,
Calling, calling,
Alone in loves sand,
Quick to sink,
Alone . . . . ,
With only time to think,
In the silence,
Lingering behind,
While I hold onto,
What is left of my mind.

With Tears

He said shut up,
Your opinion doesn't matter,
Watch the way you talk,
Or everything will shatter,
Stay away, back off,
C*** you have no brain,
When I hear what he has to say,
How does he call me insane,
He said shut up,
And I have no choice but to listen,

With tears in my eyes,
Where sorrow constantly glistens,
I say . . . God bless you,
I'm not sure about love,
Anymore, anyway,
He said shut up and just do it,
Dumb b**** you better,
Do what I say,
You better, you better,
Or things will get worse,
While the spit in his eyes reminds me,
How my God,
How can this be?

Deeper Love

Mine was a deeper love,
Deeper than just to feel,
Still there is nothing,
Nothing time cannot heal,
What is said,
Is not clear,
Still to listen,
But not always hear,
Mine was a deeper love,
The deepest ever felt,
In time, into memory,
Each day would melt,
What you say,
Every word,
Left with the echo,
Of what is heard,
Mine was a deeper love,
The kind for which I stayed pure,
Mine was a love,
And is no more.

Pray

Pray for me,
I am about to fall,
Out into empty space,

Please Jesus hear my call,
Pray for me,
I'm so confused,
Don't want to be hurt,
Or feel used,
Pray for me,
Before I sin,
I am only human,
Made of blood and skin,
Pray for me,
And all that I think,
Life will be over,
Within the eyes blink,
Pray for me,
Every angel every saint,
The pain is fierce,
And my heart beat is faint,
In the name of Jesus,
Please pray for me,
Far from perfect,
I am the best I can be.

Dead Air

The air is dead,
No movement, no sound,
Just the echo of,
A song playing around,
No its not warm,
And its comfortably dark,
Without a key,
There is nothing to unlock,
Separated from,
The atmosphere,
With a view straight,
Into the suns glare,
Resting without,
Any sleep,
The air is dead,
But my thoughts . . . . , my thoughts are deep.

Angels Song

Following the descend,
The pieces just fly,
Keeping a promise,
Not allowing it to die,
Beneath the rain,
That often falls,
While still breathing,
Through faith the spirit calls,
Sad heart and many tears,
How much more,
In that which last forever,
Resting in hope . . . , unsure,
Searching fot the good,
In what seems bad,
The things that have gone,
Stand now as what was had,
Sorrow stood at a distance,
Not far from the angels song,
Bestowing fortitude,
Vital to be strong.

Secluded

It is secluded,
Abode to be,
Its reclusive,
To abide me,
No one can,
Swallow pain as well,
I will get up,
Even though I fell,
Yes it is frigid,
But I'll exist alright,
I am adjusting to,
Empty sight,
The air is entity,
I have to embrace,
There's oblivion to remember,
And nothing to erase.

Go

Beneath the dirt,
Just adds to my pain,
You would belong to me,
No . . . never again,
Crushed, cut, bruised and torn,
Remembering the dreams,
Somehow connected,
Until now it seems,
Broken to pieces,
The promise of death,
Allowing to pass through,
Another breath,
Kissed goo bye,
Long ago in the days before,
Held in his arms,
Saying nothing more,
To go on and not speak,
A place so empty,
Far away from you,
Think back to the times,
I spent with you,
As though it were love,
It just isn't so,
Just before, just after,
Just when you go.

Pass

Pass away expire invade,
A shadow drifting beneath
The shade.

Torn Apart

Without touch,
Or even feeling,
Breathing the air,
That breath is stealing,
Kept alone,

In thw confusion,
Living life,
And its illusion,
Without freedom,
From within this cage,
Happiness struggles,
To overcome rage,
Without touch,
There is nothing to feel,
Nightmares vision,
Become so real,
To be alive,
Numb to emotion,
Inhaling the smoke,
Drinking its potion,
Time has no mercy,
Seconds no reply,
Pray, pray,
Never cry,
Words, laughter,
The beat of a heart,
Left with what,
Has not yet been torn apart.

Sharp Shooter

Bring to being,
Expose eyes to seeing,
Without intent apologize,
As the execution of tear cries,
Having no anger or hate,
For Gods help patiently wait,
A sharp shooter within,
To compete with the drive to win.

Grind

The grind of greed and jealousy,
This constant pounding noise of lies,
So patiently the poor beg and plea,
Is there no compromise?
Wedging between good and evil,

Forever this beast remains savage,
These fallen angels are seldom civil,
Still there is no relief from bondage,
As they tread on the masses to exceed,
Sometimes virtue is easily blinded by corruption,
Another heart wounded and left to bleed,
Useless the life of people thriving for destruction,
Alive their body, trapping their soul,
One too many appetites craving gold,
Over ones breath it takes control,
Cursed these emerald bills of old.

Has

Loneliness has no sound,
Emptiness has no heart,
Lost with nothing found,
Endless without a start,
To be born is taking the first breath,
Living until we are struck by death,
Sight has vision,
While the body has soul,
Thought fears indecision,
A half cannot be whole,
Falling fire upon the earth,
Tempted by hells rebirth,
Bodage restrains freedom,
As light fades to darkness,
Imagine safety surrounded by harm,
To realize the desire for more receives less,
Trapped by time to stay,
Still for the answer we pray,
Saying hello will result in good bye,
Watch as each season changes from hot to cold,
Like the sun rises and sets in the sky,
Youth eventually becomes old,

Exhausted

Exhausted with thought,
A waiting kiss,
An atmosphere,

Never before like this,
A desire to touch,
To have something real,
All embraced,
In the chance to feel,
The beating of hearts,
Combined into one,
The breath of two,
Until the rise of the sun,
Tripping over another fall,
Into a sleepless night,
Burning deep within,
Beneath the shine of the moonlight.

Rest

I am going to rest,
My head on the Lord,
Release this breath,
With the strength of a sword,
I shall thank Him,
Every day I live,
I will look for the wisdom,
In all to receive and give,
I will show kindness,
To everything He has created,
Not losing faith,
Without becoming irritated,
I am going to sleep,
Free of worry,
Because my God,
Is always with me,
I know I'm not alone,
He is a prayer away,
And in my heart Jesus,
My sweet Jesus will stay.

So Close

Lost control to a threat,
Life to live just a debt,
Lost inside all that is,

I gave God my life it is His,
Torn within and without,
What is this all about,
Existing a purpose,
So far but so close,
From crashing to flying,
Still in a breath of tears crying,
In a prayer on my knees,
Jesus help me, help me please,
Hanging from this cliff,
Echoing words . . . , What if,
Surround every doubt in love,
Resting faith in God above,
With the intention of doing right,
Calling, calling, day and night,
Left in loneliness to decide,
While what to do and not collide.

Maze

Living in the air,
As having is to need,
From the heart,
Blood rushes to bleed,
Dementia at the door,
With eyes wide open,
Watching what is done,
Listening to every word spoken,
Discerning in the hereafter,
Damned with faint praise,
Weeping bitter overthrown,
Lost in isolations maze.
Think wonder,
Felt not spoke,
Trust in time,
Run with the flow,
The color of black,
Vision our desire,
Plunge crash,
Deep within the fire,
Callapsing here,
Dreams will chase,
Left there like,
Vast wide space.

Mom

Thought I should call you,
Or maybe come by,
I seem to never get the chance,
God knows I try,
If only you knew,
What you meant to me,
Your opinions and advice,
Showing what I couldn't see,
You helped me grow,
Giving everything needed,
You lifted me up,
Until I succeeded,
You taught me about God,
And Jesus as well,
Picking me up no matter,
How many times I fell,
You show me a strength,
And a faith I wouldn't know,
You give me a love,
No one else is able to show,
Just want to thank you.
For always being there,
Giving your life to others,
So free of care,
I look up to you,
And admire you still,
I love you mom,
And always will.

Enter

Enter the day, Enter the night,
Sipping away into an endless fight,
Unfairly injected by pain,
Cluttering with thought beyond control,
Slowly eating away at the heart and soul,
Leaving the throb of hurt in the heart to remain,
Feeling the weight of life, and the gravity of bitterness,
To learn explosive emotions are better to repress,
Corrupt energy that invades this dwelling,

When perceptions are blurred demons intrude,
Hopelessly gasping for a breath of rectitude,
At times the pressure of walls closing in is compelling,
Extending lessons left unlearned,
Intense hells fire leaving only ashes burned,
Having the choice of good and evil,
To believe nothing can subdue loves power,
Though tortured by time precious each hour,
Enter; to capture what life has yet to instill.

Chains

Unlock these chains,
And all that remains,
Twisted in a mangled view,
Unprotected elegant virtue,
Unravel once done,
Dys beneath the sun,
Whispers resting in desire,
To touch if only the tip of fire,
Walking slumber precious sleep,
In fear of the company forced to keep,
While the beating heart continues to speculate,
And time races with each second unable to wait,
The dream of peace passes by,
Caught in the sight of an open eye.

Torture

You took every chance,
I had to feel.
Taught me how,
Love isn't real,
Holding on,
Kept by your side,
Waiting for something more,
Is such a lonely ride,
You could have said good bye,
You could have said we are through,
You played me like a game,
While all the time you knew,
You left me in the dark,

And said that's where I belong,
You've hurt me so much,
But God has made me strong,
Passion had so much to offer,
But I will never know,
When all you had to do,
Was let me go.

Me

I don't know where I am,
No idea where this is going,
How does one catch the wind,
While it is blowing,
There is no end in sight,
When there was not even a start,
Constantly forever,
Tearing me apart,
I don't know where I am,
No idea where this is to be,
I am helpless in Your eyes Lord,
Please . . . . please take care of me.

Time

Only if time could,
Cease for a moment,
Soundless, breathless,
Not a movement,
Not aging,
Not caging,
Wholly what is,
Completely what could be,
Left in the stillness,
With vision to see,
Leaving behind,
Escaping the mind,
Here but,
Existing not,
Caught up in,
Lifes plot,
No devotion,

Empty emotion,
Obscure strange,
Nothing to express,
It no longer matters,
More or less,
Words none to subdue,
Yet no question or clue,
There is no good,
Nor bad,
No reason for content,
Or being sad,
Just time and its tick,
So sophistic

Blue

The sun is rising,
And I haven't slept,
From a night of dreams,
Once more I am kept,
I look for reasons,
But come out with rhyme,
Trying to get the most of,
This every dy race with time,
The sun is rising,
And there is nothing I can do,
My eyes won't shut,
And the sky is turning blue.

Silence

Silence has me,
Within its grip,
Thoughts like a,
Faucet drip, drip,
Another taste of,
Sadness to sip,
Loneliness has me,
Within its view,
It's taking away,
Not helping me through,
Sometimes unaware,

All that is done to undo,
Despair has me,
Within its squeeze,
Standing alone in,
Depressions breeze.

Driveway

Here I am,
At your door,
I came to say hi . . . ,
But I am not sure,
I'll sit here,
With the memories,
Surrounded by your love,
And the view of country trees,
Guess I can stay,
For just a few minutes more,
Even though I know,
Know you would not answer,
No you won't answer the door,
Here I am . . . . ,
Just wanted to say hi . . . ,
But all there is left to do,
Is drive away and cry.

You Are

You are the reason,
I possess to live,
And have taught me,
What it means to give,
You are the high,
Bestowing hope,
To relieve the stress,
Which allows me to cope,
You are the time,
That is never wasted,
The sweetest kiss,
I have ever tasted,
You are the hand,
I reach to hold,

A body of fire,
When it is cold,
You are every beat,
Within my heart,
And of my love,
The truest part.

Undying

She feels as if in a dream,
To her this emotion might seem,
To him passion is an undying stare,
Two hearts surrendering to the atmosphere,
Acting within the heart instead of the mind,
A vision at times said to be blind,
Watching as she sips on this powerful potion,
His words unspoken come through with each motion,
Captured time enchant their moment,
Silent her touch thinking from heaven he was sent,
As deeper they sink into this sea of burning fire,
Becoming one they are pulled into the waves by desire,
A forgiveness that knows no wrong,
Altering the delicate to become strong,
Enduring her imprint within his soul to ingrain,
While upon her lips left his kiss forever to remain.

Destiny

My destiny,
Is to die,
Death will come,
And I'll say goo bye,
Put away the days gone by,
I'll look through,
The eyes of my soul,
Fighting with all my strength,
Until I reach my goal,
Doing my best but there is no control,
I'll shake the grim reapers hand,
Stepping without my flesh, my body,
Looking down . . . . ,
It will be . . .

It will be me,
Releasing every emotion,
Memories no longer there,
No I won't and,
Don't have to care,
All who pass come through here,
I will embrace,
The angel of death,
Until I rest in peace,
Until my last breath,
I will say my final prayer,
In the name of Jesus and in love,
I will ask for forgiveness,
From almighty God above,
And then fly away . . . , with the wings of a dove.

Unknown

Inside a whisper,
Into stars wishes thrown,
While dreams dance,
Within the skies unknown.

Bullet

The ringing in my ears,
Please make it stop,
The falling of tears,
Each and every drop,
Thinking in vivid color,
Surrounded and devoured,
Shaking and weak,
In a corner like a coward,
Outside looking in,
Inside looking out,
What does trust,
Owe to doubt,
Waking up to sleep,
Sleeping to wake,
Picking apart perfect,
Praising a mistake,
When living is to die,

And dying is to live,
Emptiness . . . . ,
Fails to give,
As torture waits to hurt,
And hurt continues to torture,
Left with a disease,
That has no cure,
Spinning the barrel as a game,
Of Russian roulette
Pulling the trigger,
To fire a blank or a bullet.

Success

Waking up I'm alone,
With a stillness,
Enough to drive one mad,
Losing blood, but fearless,
Honoring what is left,
Left of passions endurance,
Fading out, fading out,
No longer as to make an appearance,
Waking up . . . . ,
Wisdom honed to razor sharpness,
Driven towards dreams,
To become a victim of success.

Soul

As we wander from reality,
We can see the motion of a vision set free,
To such unique concept refined,
The soul surrenders deeply,
We are all prisoners to the heart and mind,
Surging through emotions potent enough to blind,
For the moment we capture impulsive insight,
As we slip away from pressures confined,
Aware of thoughts colliding colors day and night,
Timeless the conscious who is lost in flight,
We acknowledge death as the ruler of every human fate,
Still mental insanity to everyone at one point remains a fight,

The strength of the mind has the power to isolate,
In a place where the spirit of moods and emotions initiate,
Causing the flow of imagination,
While our souls thrive on what we create.

Dream

Slipping into slumber my eyes calmly close,
Drifting further and further into a depthless doze,
Watching pictures in my mind begin to propose,
As the soul becomes lost in all that comes and goes,
Helplessly carried off in emotions highs and lows,
In search of where imagination flows,
Escaping from time that has not yet froze,
Still the spirit and flesh never divide,
Yet I crash through colors that collide,
As the vision of logic breaches wide,
Listening to the laughter and pain while I have cried,
The subconscious steps through doorways that decide,
Temporarily taken beyond from inside,
Only to ask "why" dreams have lied.

Sleep

I sleep across,
Two kitchen chairs,
Furthermore sadness,
Beyond crying tears,
Kept to be benevolent,
Made to consider how others feel,
Decaying flesh, confusion,
To discern between false and real,
Limited to what is allowed,
Within isolations cage,
Loves disturbing embrace,
Words arranged on another page,
As years of trust,
Stares back at me with a grin and wink,
Wisdom is on guard,
Fearing what to think,
Realizing all I was not,

Intended to know,
Obligated sufficient,
Determined to go.

Emotion

An open heart,
Has no protection,
Absent nowhere,
Pursuing direction,
Like time spaces,
The moon from the sun,
Escaping to adjust,
Into images however which run,
No . . . the heart,
Does not withstand a shield,
Married, divorced,
Or playing the field,
Love is not a game,
Or a fairytale,
Empathy enigma,
To come to be,
The satisfied desire,
Aligning emotions anarchy.

Thankful

I have been kicked,
Slapped in the face,
Punched in the stomach,
And made to feel out of place,
In return I worked harder,
But still am called names,
Again and again I turned the other cheek,
Not to play these games,
'I've been deceived by relatives,
I thought would care,
But found God keeps me safe,
Because I never miss a day of prayer,
I have been pushed,
And pushed aside,
With pain at times,

Difficult to hide,
Felt so alone,
Confused about where to belong,
However continue to live,
As though nothing is wrong,
I've been scared and hurt,
By people I have trusted,
A victim of their sleight,
And am somewhat disgusted,
Yet I am thankful,
For God has blessed me,
With the strength to endure,
Who I am and am to be.

Rust

Don't know where to run,
Or who to trust,
Like metal that,
Builds with rust,
Tripping on my,
Own two feet,
So much in my life,
Labeled incomplete,
I'm on my knees,
Begging for relief,
Suffocating on my breath,
As if air was a thief.

Forlorn

I'm going looney in this bin,
On a forlorn helpless drift,
Can you imagine?
Being lost in times unconscious gift,
Feeling the bitter loosened screw,
Twisting into my identity,
While fixed on an empty view,
I clutch tight to sanity,
Passing through thid cold and lonely gloom,
Of uncontrolled mental torment,
Where darkness is to consume,

Clouding all that is innocent,
Given another lie without a destination,
Inflicting my reckless attitude,
Triggered by a responsible isolation,
As I try not to give into worthless tears that intrude,
I rest in ambition intensely confined,
My mouth moves yet nothing is spoken,
My eyes can see, yet I am blind,
Leaving my confiding heart blamelessly broken.

Digress

I digress into immortal,
Seemingly just at last,
Running through,
Dwelling upon telecast,
Not admitting dejection,
A soldier to duty,
Uninterrupted focus,
To infringe upon ambiguity,
From careless refuge,
Happiness overthrown,
Cast down beyond blame,
Reminded of the emptiness I own,
Love scatters in the wind,
Uncertain to predict,
A passage entering mental impression,
Waiting for what wisdom has to inflict,
Constantly criticized,
The heart selects with caution,
Without choice comply,
Brutally beaten by emotion.

Done

Did you hold her in your arms,
When tears feel from her eyes,
Did you get so involved,
As another piece of us dies,
Do you think of sin,
And where life has lead,
While concept of her,

Lying next to me in bed,
I'm not done with you yet,
Did she hear that too,
You did the same with me,
Does she have a clue,
Did you embrace and kiss her,
Asking if she was okay,
Was she like me? Always's ready, wanting more,
Please . . . tell me what another man's wife would say,
Did you leave what we had,
So far behind,
While I was home with three babies,
Must have slipped your mind,
Did she say not to go,
When it was time to leave her side,
Pulling her in for another kiss,
I am done . . . . hope you're satisfied.

Palliate

Into perpetual success,
Not settling for les,
Articulate, with exactness,
To cease living fallacious,
In the depths dexterous,
As fear breathes cautious,
Discarding the insipid,
A metaphor of did,
Breaking intellect morbid,
Within the period of existence,
Withdrawing obedience,
Below the deluge of silence,
To finally select and fluctuate,
Looming accurate,
While echos in the air palliate.

Okay

Its okay,
It will be alright,
Close your eyes,
Sleep for the night,

Hold yourself together,
Just another day,
Get on your knees,
Because it is time to pray,
Its okay,
It will be alright,
Crawl from the darkness,
Into the light,
Emptiness shall fade,
Emotions will melt,
Forgiveness and love,
Overtaking all that is felt,
Its okay,
It will be alright,
Held within the jaw,
Of hurts bite,
There is no answer,
For the pain here,
Kept in a promise,
A promise I fear,
Its okay, It will be alright,
Take a deep breath,
And hold on tight.

Mmmiss you

I have not the day,
Nor even the night,
Still the echo,
It will be alright,
I have not the time,
Nor a minute to spare,
The hours go by,
But do not care,
Captured by,
All that captures me,
My eyes they are open,
But it's so hard to see,

See

I learned not to,
Get lost in feeling,
That there might be,
A chance for healing,
I can see there is,
No happily ever after,
Yeah it was funny,
Left in your laughter,
Special to me the only one,
I hope, I hope you had your fun,
Cause I am, I am done,
I accepted your desire,
Was not for me,
You could have at least,
Set me free,
You taught me to,
Be so strong,
I no longer cry,
When I hear our song,
That tears are,
A waste of time,
Hope you like where I used to be,
I won't listen to your plea,
Cause you did not hear me,
I used to wait for you,
When you came home late,
Now for time alone,
I can't wait.

Passage

Lionhearted byword,
A spectator to ratify,
Connected in sequence,
To good honor comply,
To embark upon peace,
Beyond doubt enduring virginity,
A metaphor perplexing,
On the verge of the psyche,
To intrigue with a passage,

A soldier to solitude,
Breaking through the clouds,
As foreshadows intrude.

Deranged

To fade away is, good bye,
Returning never or even so,
Equal in value to further try,
Who is to know,
Too deranged to lay eyes upon why?
For the moment I'll tolerate it to go,
In the midst of a sigh,
Barely existing good purpose show,
To what end assuming passions lie,
In other words beyond measure slow,
Extending to justify,
It makes no difference as far as I owe,
Without exception you I cry,
Meeting head on supported by the blow,
While uncertain vision hangs on like grim death,
Stealing what is left of my breath.

B - Jean

Skin on skin,
Softly biting on your lip,
Tongue to tongue,
Your hand on my hip,
Breathing heavy,
Even when I'm alone.
Like the excitement,
Building within a moan,
Touching my stomach,
Pulling on my shirt,
A feeling so sublime,
To the extent of hurt,
The loss of balance,
Passion causing flesh to shake,
There are no words,
Only desires ache.

Halfway

Persisting beloved emptiness,
Obscurity by silence,
Emitting the last breath of a promise,
At heart rending expense,
Grasping onto words,
Arranged in a prayer,
Because when I am alone,
God is the only one there,
Exploited thought,
Damaged by time,
Breath as short,
As a rhyme,
Halfway to heaven,
Halfway to hell,
With no key to open,
The door of this cell.

Boundaries

Frozen not beyond the boundaries of unseen fear,
Separated only through atmosphere,
A disembodied spirit misplaced with the time of flight,
Dwelling heavily upon the darken shades of night,
Captured in the glimpse touching the eye,
The well known shadows ascending by,
Vanishing a whisper of unexplained sound,
Somehow escaping the buried ground,
Incapable of happiness or even hurt,
The ones heaven and hell chose to desert,
Did they not endure enough pain,
AS a slamming door seized this thought,
If they are deceased is life really short?

Know

You thought,
I'd be crying,
Thinking you could hurt me,
By being cold and lying,

To save myself,
I left you behind,
Numb to the pain,
Not to lose my mind,
Surrounded by nothing leaving all that began,
Pushing me to run,
So I ran . . . . I ran,
I thought you understood,
I thought there was love,
Invisible to you,
I wasn't thought of,
Holding me as if,
You'd never let me go,
You helped me to learn,
Now I know.

This Sky

Silence the heartless,
To all in need,
While tears and sorrow
Off hurt will feed,
As a reflection,
Reflects what is in its sight,
Darkness would fill,
The sky without light,
Thinking about time,
And how it slips away,
Life depends on seconds,
Day by day,
While nothing in,
Its path is new,
Not even this sky,
This sky of blue.

Live

My God I want to live,
Before I die,
Make every minute count,
That goes by,
Dance to the sound,

Of music every day,
To be heard when,
I have something to say,
To escape the sadness,
That tries to seep,
Only having good dreams,
When I am asleep,
To live life to the best,
Of my ability,
To make good,
Of the bad I see.

Mine

Let the words flow,
Emotions in ink,
Feel the wind blow,
As I deeply think,
Blessed the talent,
To express and rhyme,
Many of my hours are spent,
Reflecting sometimes less,
Watching as emotions run wild,
Through the eye of the mind,
Some are warm and mild,
And some are cruel and unkind,
With my senses flowing free,
Words pour as smooth as wine,
Written for all to see,
An image that is mine.
As clouds in the way,
It hinders the sun,
Like nothing to play,
The game is over and done,
Years of love,
Left with none,
Demons stealing control,
When life is to own,
As a bird to a safe realm,
It has flown,
While unto the breeze,
Each page is blown,
Conforming what is,

And shall be,
With no choice,
But to wait and see,
Aware death leads,
To life's eternity,
As a cloud,
Occluding plain sight,
Deep as the dark,
Darkness of the night,
Like pulling the trigger,
Fires to ignite,
The heart it suffers,
Alone inside,
Where the benevolence,
Of tears once cried,
Like a careless story,
That has lied.

Air

It's like falling back,
With nothing there,
Hoping to be caught,
In mid-air.

Sun

In a loss for words,
Heavens so far away,
Forced not to feel,
Holding every prayer to pray,
All I thought I knew,
Leaves me unsure,
Without a clue,
In the middle of a breath,
Shades of evening in a stare,
With vision just to be,
Wither away in it's own fear,
Like the beauty within,
The colors of each flower,
As the dryness of the dirt,
So needs a shower,

Time goes on,
With the might of a storm,
Like the sun,
Love should be warm.

Lost

Lost control to a threat,
Life to live just a debt,
Lost inside all that is,
I gave God my life it is His,
Torn within and without,
What is this all about,
Existing a purpose,
So far, but so close,
From crashing to flying,
Still in a breath of tears crying,
In a prayer on my knees,
Jesus help me please,
Hanging from this cliff,
Echoing words "What If",
Surround all doubt in love,
Resting faith in God above,
With the intention of doing right,
Calling, calling, day and night,
Left in the loneliness to decide,
While what to do and not collide.

Ache

Living with demons,
Though no hate run through these veins,
All there is . . . . is faith,
To take away these pains,
There are only words,
Thoughts that run through the head,
Remembering not to always believe,
What has been said,
Waiting for the light,
The tunnel that leads to,
The end of the night,
Never to enter the doorway,

In which weakness hides,
Only to depend on,
What strength provides,
Relying on the next,
Breath to take,
The heart is meant to beat,
Not ache.

Cry

Don't know if I should cry,
Or be relieved,
The only good thing is,
No one was deceived,
And each and every time,
You walked away,
If you only knew,
How I hoped you'd stay,
You gave me thoughts,
To risk it all,
To embrace the sin,
Into its trap trip and fall,
Not sure if I should feel hurt,
Or even be glad,
When another's love,
It's not mine to be had.

Fades

Within the wisdom,
Of a tear,
Experience reaches out,
To pain through fear,
Left in the darkness,
Of nothing there,
Lost in the time,
Each minute would spare,
Held in the words,
Of a prayer,
As every whisper,
Fades into the air.

Weak

Save me from myself,
Weak as I could be,
Advertising emotion,
Saving empathy,
Praying for strength
Fragile from neglect,
Going through the motion,
What did empty hours expect,
Complicated by thought,
Trying to keep it all straight,
With the words repeating,
Good things come to those who wait,
How long, how long,
God life is passing by,
Minutes become a strain,
Lost not understanding why,
Save me from myself,
I am only made of dust,
Helpless to feelings,
You can and cannot trust,
Dividing wrong from right,
Within confusion of the mind,
Sometimes to see,
Sometimes left blind.

Be There

Hear my voice,
When no one is around,
Listen as I whisper,
Involve yourself in its sound,
See me at your side,
When no one is there,
Hold me close,
So I can show you how I care,
Feel my arms around you,
On your worst day,
If there are tears,
Allow me to wipe them away,
I'll be the comfort,

When there is pain,
I'll be there for you,
Again and again.

Ambition

Armed with ambition,
Into meaning thoughts perish,
Focus not to,
Not to diminish,
Comprehensive and abstract,
Held in a logical view,
Black ash not beyond sight,
Leading to wisdoms rescue,
Still what good is knowing,
Without the ability to create,
Descending cipher,
Fragile to the force of fate,
Moving without effort,
Through and with erudite,
So beyond recognition here,
An oddity ready to ignite,
Existing with an evening song,
Humble, a disposition ornate,
A state of being on fire,
Absorbing and articulate.

Extending

Spoken in words,
Extending from the heart,
As the eyes of a panther,
Luminate in the dark,
Into which thoughts reflect,
In the direction of perseptive,
Apparent the blueprint of time,
Through speculation live,
Spilling over resolve,
To deluge in torque,
Like a road,
Coming to a fork,
Based upon determination,

Avoiding defiance that invades,
As morbid solitude rest beneath,
The shadow of its shade.

Until

Like the past,
You can leave it behind,
But there is no safety from,
What follows and reminds,
Do what you want,
And it will hunt you down,
It will cause your head,
To spin around and round,
Like the past,
It doesn't come back,
Nothing can be changed,
As pictures in a stack,
Memories are always there,
As large as the sky,
Time only pushes ahead,
Until it is . . . it is good bye.

Rage

He has a rage,
I try to keep calm,
It is safe now,
No reason for alarm,
I won't talk,
Or have a say,
Everything we do,
Is . . . . his way,
I won't feel,
Or even cry,
My opinion means nothing,
And I never ask him why,
I keep to myself,
And mind my business,
Because you can wake anger,
By simply answering no or yes,
I won't laugh,

Not sure it's funny,
I'm not allowed to be involved,
With bills and money,
I always think,
Before I act,
I'll work it out,
Not to get smacked,
How can I leave,
There is so much at risk,
To avoid him,
Using his fist,
I won't argue,
I never fight,
I am wrong,
He is right.

Beyond

Beyond the gray,
And drops of rain,
Held in a breath,
Laughter whispers pain,
Resting within,
The beat of a heart,
The putting together,
Of what was falling apart.

Pushed

I pushed thought,
So far back,
It never stops,
The constant attack,
Like Mick Jagger said Paint it black,
As the wind,
That rustles the leaves,
All that is important,
Stolen, taken by thieves,
In a place where only a fool believes,
There is no wound deeper,
Than one of the heart alone and unsure,
Love has no measure,

Nor hate found a cure,
Emptiness has forsaken,
An artic lonely nothing there,
Without the ability to listen,
No one is able to hear,
As sadness drips from the eye as a tear.

Obstacles

In life so many,
Things can go wrong,
Obstacles are there,
To make one strong,
Dust off, pick it up,
Breath is worth more,
Cease recollection,
Of what happened before,
Be glad for the moment,
Live for today,
Do not give in to worry,
And you'll find your way.

Thank You

I want to thank you for,
The love I didn't get,
And tell me again how lucky,
I am that we met,
I want to thank you,
For believing in me,
For the slap in the face,
Of reality,
For the emptiness,
I didn't need to feel,
And for the passion,
I thought was real,
It left me alone,
With more time to pray,
To further my faith,
Bringing me closer to God every day,
Thank you for the painful words,
That caused an ache in my heart,

Leaving me in emotion,
To tear myself apart.

Divine

Lacking intellectual depth,
Analytical alienation,
Unwelcome mental preparation,
Resourceful and awakened,
Emerging as an angels song,
Scattering in the winds,
Taken to the heart where to belong,
Embarking upon,
Credible words in compline,
Clever imbues initiate,
Flourishing divine.
Be quiet eat the hurt,
As mud is made of,
Water and dirt,
Is there something,
That will save,
Why would it need more,
Than what Jesus gave,
Alone because of,
All the signals sent,
Life is temporarily,
Precious time spent,
Like the air,
Without a breeze,
Left in what the past,
Recalls as memories,
I don't know where I am,
Lost in existence,
How then can this be?
Sorrow into words or a sentence.

Think

I'll think of you,
With each breath,
Brought to life,
Then put to death,

Sit by myself,
With only these words,
Believing one day,
To be heard,
Among the gift of God,
Embracing all that I see,
Living and breathing,
The heart inside of me,
In the mist of the soul,
Searching for more,
I'll think of you,
And how it was before.

Printed in the United States
By Bookmasters